this

JOURNAL

belongs to

....

....

Keep on the sunny side, always on the sunny side,
Keep on the sunny side of life;
It will help us every day, it will brighten all the way
If we keep on the sunny side of life.

ADA BLENKHORN

"Keep on the Sunny Side of Life" is a hymn written in 1899 in response to a young man wanting his wheelchair pushed on the sunny side of the street. It has become a perennial favorite crooned in concerts and over the airwaves for more than one hundred years. The message is an endearing reminder that choosing the sunny side of life is always an option.

Hatch Show Print has been a Nashville icon since the 1800s, and continues to thrive as a working letterpress poster and design shop today, creating artwork with the same printing methods they have used for more than a century. Their printed posters and handbills have celebrated a wide distribution through music, political, and big-name events.

The combination of Hatch Show Print's iconic design and the beloved lyrics from "The Sunny Side of Life," along with inspirational quotes and verses, provides a wonderfully creative space for journalers and songwriters, sketch artists and doodlers to let their light shine.

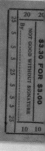

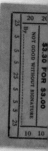

Isn't it a wonderful morning? The world looks like
something God had just imagined for His own pleasure.

LUCY MAUD MONTGOMERY

A cheerful friend is like a sunny day, which sheds its brightness on all around.

SIR JOHN LUBBOCK

Open wide the windows of our spirits
and fill us full of light.

CHRISTINA ROSSETTI

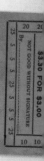

All things are possible for one who believes.

THE BIBLE

Be such a person, and live such a life, that if every one were such as you, and every life a life such as yours, this earth would be God's paradise.

PHILLIPS BROOKS

God's bright sunshine overhead,
God's flowers beside your feet...
And by such pleasant pathways led,
May all your life be sweet.

HELEN WAITHMAN

Wherever you go, no matter what the weather,
always bring your own sunshine.

ANTHONY J. D'ANGELO

Imagination is the highest kite one can fly.
LAUREN BACALL

I can do everything through Christ, who gives me strength.

THE BIBLE

I wish you sunshine on your path and storms to season your journey. I wish you peace—in the world in which you live and in the smallest corner of the heart where truth is kept.

ROBERT A. WARD

Live for today but hold your hands open to tomorrow.
Anticipate the future and its changes with joy.

BARBARA JOHNSON

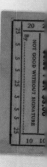

God is the sunshine that warms us, the rain that melts the
frost and waters the young plants. The presence of God is
a climate of strong and bracing love, always there.

JOAN ARNOLD

· ·

· ·

· ·

· ·

· ·

· ·

· ·

· ·

· ·

· ·

· ·

· ·

· ·

Sunshine is a matter of attitude.

F. W. BOREHAM

No eye has seen, no ear has heard, and no mind has imagined what God has prepared for those who love him.

We need to recapture the power of imagination;
we shall find that life can be full of wonder, mystery,
beauty, and joy.

SIR HAROLD SPENCER JONES

Your own sky will lighten,
If other skies you brighten
By just being happy
With a heart full of song.

RIPLEY D. SAUNDERS

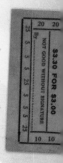

*Friends splash our world with sunny color
and set our hearts to flight.*

JANET L. SMITH

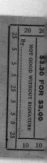

Keep your face to the sunshine
and you cannot see the shadows.

HELEN KELLER

Then they cried out to the LORD in their trouble,
and he brought them out of their distress.
He stilled the storm to a whisper;
the waves of the sea were hushed.

THE BIBLE

A positive spirit is like a sunny day;
it sheds a brightness over everything;
it sweetens our circumstances and soothes our souls.

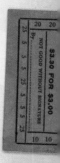

"Just living is not enough," said the butterfly. "One must have sunshine, freedom, and a little flower."

HANS CHRISTIAN ANDERSEN

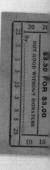

A joyful heart is like a sunshine of God's love,
the hope of eternal happiness, a burning flame of God.

MOTHER TERESA

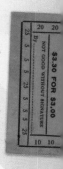

Those who bring sunshine to the lives of others
cannot keep it from themselves.

SIR JAMES M. BARRIE

From the rising of the sun to its setting,
the name of the LORD is to be praised!

THE BIBLE

There's a dark and a troubled side of life
There's a bright and a sunny side, too
Tho' we meet with the darkness and strife
The sunny side we also may view.

ADA BLENKHORN

Thank You, Father, for the beautiful surprises you are planning for me today. So often in my life, when it looked like the day would be dismal, depressing, dark, an unexpected burst of golden sunshine exploded through a black cloud, sending inspiring shafts of warm, beautiful sunshine into my life.

ROBERT SCHULLER

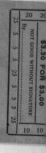

May dazzling rays of sunshine reach through the clouds and brighten up your skies.

*Into all our lives, in many simple, familiar,
homely ways, God infuses this element of joy from
the surprises of life, which unexpectedly brighten
our days, and fill our eyes with light.*

SAMUEL LONGFELLOW

. . . .

. . . .

. . . .

. . . .

. . . .

. . . .

. . . .

. . . .

. . . .

. . . .

. . . .

. . . .

. . . .

. . . .

. . . .

The ways of right-living people glow with light;
the longer they live, the brighter they shine.

THE BIBLE

How wonderful it is that nobody need wait a single moment before starting to improve the world.

ANNE FRANK

Some days, it is enough encouragement just to watch the clouds break up and disappear, leaving behind a blue patch of sky and bright sunshine that is so warm upon my face. It's a glimpse of divinity; a kiss from heaven.

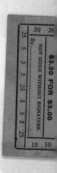

Green pastures are before me,
Which yet I have not seen;
Bright skies will soon be o'er me,
Where the dark clouds have been.

ANNA LAETITIA WARING

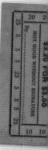

*There may be times in your life when it all seems dark
and you cannot see or trace the hand of God, but yet God
is working. Just as much as He works in the bright sunlight,
He works all through the night.*

The LORD will guide you always;
he will satisfy your needs in a sun-scorched land.

THE BIBLE

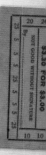

. . . .

. . . .

. . . .

. . . .

. . . .

. . . .

. . . .

. . . .

. . . .

. . . .

. . . .

. . . .

. . . .

. . . .

. . . .

Allow your dreams a place in your prayers and plans.
God-given dreams can help you move into the future
He is preparing for you.

BARBARA JOHNSON

The soft, sweet summer was warm and glowing,
Bright were the blossoms on every bough:
I trust Him when the roses were blooming;
I trust Him now....

L. B. COWMAN

*Those who live on the mountain have a longer day
than those who live in the valley. Sometimes all we need
to brighten our day is to rise a little higher.*

S. J. BARROWS

What sunshine is to flowers, smiles are to humanity.

JOSEPH ADDISON

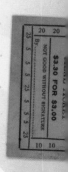

LORD…*may all who love you be like the sun when it rises in its strength.*

THE BIBLE

God's grand, limitless imagination spills into everything.

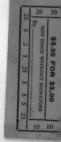

Love comforts like sunshine after the rain.

WILLIAM SHAKESEPEARE

Be on the lookout for mercies. The more we look for them,
the more of them we will see. Blessings brighten
when we count them.

MALTBIE D. BABCOCK

One taper lights a thousand,
Yet shines as it has shone;
And the humblest light may kindle
A brighter than its own.

HEZEKIAH BUTTERWORTH

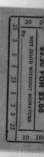

I recommend having fun, because there is nothing better for people in this world than to eat, drink, and enjoy life. That way they will experience some happiness along with all the hard work God gives them under the sun.

THE BIBLE

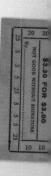

He made you so you could share in His creation,
could love and laugh and know Him.

TED GRIFFEN

There is no danger of developing eyestrain from looking on the bright side of things.

*Life is no brief candle to me. It is a...splendid torch...
and I want to make it burn as brightly as possible before
handing it over to future generations.*

GEORGE BERNARD SHAW

. . . .

. . . .

. . . .

. . . .

. . . .

. . . .

. . . .

. . . .

. . . .

. . . .

. . . .

. . . .

. . . .

. . . .

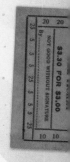

This bright, new day, complete with twenty-four hours
of opportunities, choices, and attitudes comes with a
perfectly matched set of 1,440 minutes. This unique gift,
this one day, cannot be exchanged, replaced, or refunded.
Handle with care. Make the most of it.

The sunrise shall visit us from on high to give light
to those who sit in darkness and in the shadow of death,
to guide our feet into the way of peace.

THE BIBLE

God is love; His mercy brightens
All the path in which we rove;
Bliss He wakes and woe He lightens:
God is wisdom, God is love.

SIR JOHN BOWRING

*Our Creator would never have made such lovely days,
and given us the deep hearts to enjoy them, above and
beyond all thought, unless we were meant to be immortal.*

NATHANIEL HAWTHORNE

Tho' the storm in its fury breaks today,
Crushing hopes that we cherished so dear;
Storm and cloud will in time pass away,
The sun again will shine bright and clear.

ADA BLENKHORN

Good humor is a tonic for mind and body. It is the best antidote for anxiety and depression. It is a business asset. It attracts and keeps friends. It lightens human burdens.

GRENVILLE KLEISER

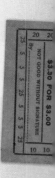

Take delight in the LORD, *and he will give you*
the desires of your heart.

THE BIBLE

DROP THIS STUB IN BOX

NAME

ADDRESS

PHONE

N.º   401

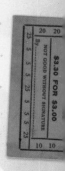

*Begin today! No matter how feeble the light, let it shine
as best it may. The world may need just that quality
of light which you have.*

HENRY C. BLINN

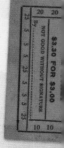

The world looks brighter from behind a smile.

If we pray, we will become that sunshine of God's love—
in our own home, the place where we live,
and in the world at large.

MOTHER TERESA

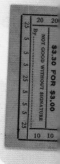

The inner half of every cloud
Is bright and shining;
I therefore turn my clouds about,
And always wear them inside out
To show the lining.

ELLEN THORNEYCROFT FOWLER

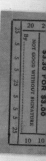

If you are filled with light, with no dark corners,
then your whole life will be radiant, as though a floodlight
were filling you with light.

THE BIBLE

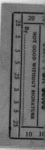

*Always be in a state of expectancy, and see that
you leave room for God to come in as He likes.*

OSWALD CHAMBERS

*Wise is the person who can take the little moment
as it comes and make it brighter before its gone.*

DANIEL ORCUTT

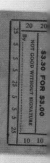

Farther along we'll know all about it;
Farther along we'll understand why.
Cheer up my brothers, live in the sunshine,
We'll understand it all by and by.

SOUTHERN GOSPEL HYMN

Humor is one of God's most marvelous gifts.... Humor makes our heavy burdens light and smooths the rough spots in our pathways.

SAM ERVIN

It is you who light my lamp; the LORD my God
lightens my darkness.

THE BIBLE

Go confidently in the direction of your dreams!
Live the life you've imagined.

HENRY DAVID THOREAU

The day is done, the sun has set,
Yet light still tints the sky;
My heart stands still
In reverence,
For God is passing by.

RUTH ALLA WAGER

. . . .

. . . .

. . . .

. . . .

. . . .

. . . .

. . . .

. . . .

. . . .

. . . .

. . . .

. . . .

. . . .

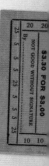

Who cares about the clouds when we're together?
Just sing a song and bring the sunny weather.

DALE EVANS

A good laugh is sunshine in a house.

WILLIAM MAKEPEACE THACKERAY

I will brighten the darkness before them and smooth out the road ahead of them. Yes, I will indeed do these things; I will not forsake them.

THE BIBLE

When I need a dose of wonder I wait for a clear night
and go look for the stars.... Often the wonder of the stars
is enough to return me to God's loving grace.

MADELEINE L'ENGLE

A cloudy day is no match for a sunny disposition.
WILLIAM ARTHUR WARD

*Go outside, to the fields, enjoy nature and the sunshine,
go out and try to recapture happiness in yourself
and in God. Think of all the beauty that's still left
in and around you and be happy!*

ANNE FRANK

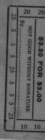

When we bring sunshine into the lives of others,
we're warmed by it ourselves.

BARBARA JOHNSON

Your sun will never set again,
and your moon will wane no more;
the Lord will be your everlasting light,
and your days of sorrow will end.

THE BIBLE

Dear Lord, grant me the grace of wonder. Surprise me,
amaze me, awe me in every crevice of Your universe.

ABRAHAM JOSHUA HESCHEL

In this big wide world of ours,
God has made enough sunshine
For everyone to have a share,
Sometime...Somewhere.

ZELDA DAVIS HOWARD

What we are is God's gift to us.
What we become is our gift to God.

ELEANOR POWELL

Let us greet with a song of hope each day,
Tho' the moments be cloudy or fair,
Let us trust in our Saviour alway,
Who keepeth everyone in His care.

ADA BLENKHORN

Ellie Claire® Gift & Paper Expressions
Franklin TN, 37067
Ellie Claire is registered trademark of Worthy Media, Inc.

Keep on the Sunny Side of Life Journal
© 2016 by Ellie Claire
Artwork © 2016 Hatch Show Print. Used under license, all rights reserved.
Published by Ellie Claire, an imprint of Worthy Publishing Group, a division of Worthy Media, Inc.

ISBN 978-1-60936-960-6

Stock or custom editions of Ellie Claire titles may be purchased in bulk for educational, business, ministry, fundraising, or sales promotional use. For information, please e-mail info@EllieClaire.com

Cover and interior design by Hatch Show Print | www.hatchshowprint.com

Printed in China

1 2 3 4 5 6 7 8 9 – 21 20 19 18 17 16